TRADITIONAL
FAIRY TALES

Classic bedtime stories

TRADITIONAL
FAIRY TALES

Classic bedtime stories

Illustrated by Annie-Claude Martin

TRANSEDITION

French-language edition:
© 2005 by Éditions Nathan, Paris, France

Illustrations by Annie-Claude Martin

English language edition:
© 2005 Transedition Ltd

ISBN 1 898250 12 X

Printed and bound in China

CONTENTS

(All tales have been retold)

Little Red Riding Hood

Once upon a time there was a little village girl, the prettiest you have ever seen. Her mother loved her dearly, as did her grandmother. She had made her a little red hood which suited her so well that everyone called her Little Red Riding Hood.

One day her mother said to her, "Your grandmother is not very well. Go and see how she is – you can take her some cookies and this homemade jar of jelly."

Little Red Riding Hood left right away to visit her grandmother who lived in another village. As she was walking through the forest she met a wolf. He would have liked to gobble her up on the spot, but he did not dare to because there were some woodcutters nearby in the forest. He pretended to be very kind and asked her where she was going.

The poor girl did not know that it was dangerous to talk to a wolf and she said to him, "I am going to see my grandmother, to take her some cookies and a jar of jelly my mother made for her."

"Does she live very far away?" asked the wolf.

"Oh yes," replied Little Red Riding Hood, "her house is beyond the mill, by the first house in the village."

"Well," said the wolf. "I would like to see her too. I will take this road here, and you take the other road, and we will see who arrives first."

The wolf set off on the shortest path, running as fast as he could, while the little girl went by the other, longer path, amusing herself by gathering nuts, running after butterflies and picking small bunches of flowers.

It did not take the wolf very long to reach the grandmother's house.

He reached up and knocked at the door.

Tap, tap.

"Who is it?" came a voice from inside.

"It is your granddaughter, Little Red Riding Hood," said the wolf, disguising his voice. "I have brought you some cookies and a jar of jelly my mother has made for you."

The good grandmother, who was in bed, called out, "Lift up the latch and come in."

The wolf lifted the latch and the door opened.

At once he leapt on to the bed and ate up the poor woman in less than a second! Then he closed the door and laid down in the grandmother's bed to wait for Little Red Riding Hood

A few moments later she knocked at the door.

Tap, tap.

"Who is it?" came the gruff wolf's voice.

When she heard this Little Red Riding Hood was a little scared at first, but remembering her grandmother was ill she answered, "It is your granddaughter, Little Red Riding Hood. I've brought you some cookies and a jar of jelly my mother has made for you."

The wolf softened his voice a little and called out, "Lift up the latch and come in."

Little Red Riding Hood lifted the latch and the door opened.

The wolf hid under the bed covers and said, "Put the cookies and the jar of jelly on the table, and come sit on the bed beside me."

Little Red Riding Hood climbed on to the bed and stared at her grandmother.

"Grandma, what big arms you have!" she cried.

"All the better to hug you with," the wolf replied.

"And Grandma, what big ears you have!"

"All the better to hear you with."

"Grandma, what big eyes you have!"

"All the better to see you with, my child."

"Grandma, what big teeth you have!" cried Little Red Riding Hood.

"All the better to eat you with!" barked the wolf and, throwing back the covers, he leapt out of bed.

Just as he was about to eat up the little girl, the woodcutter who had been in the forest burst into the cottage. With one blow of his axe he cut off the wolf's head and nobody was ever troubled by that wicked creature again.

Hansel and Gretel

At the edge of a vast forest lived a poor wood-cutter with his wife and their two children. The little boy was called Hansel and the little girl Gretel, and the family were so poor they had hardly anything to eat. Even worse, a great famine was threatening the land and the woodcutter was finding it very hard to make a living.

One evening, when the children had gone to bed, the man sighed and said to his wife, "What is to become of us? How are we going to feed our children when we don't even have anything for ourselves?"

"Well, I have a good idea," answered his wife. "Tomorrow, early in the morning, we will take the children to the thickest and darkest place in the forest. We will light a fire for them and give them each a piece of bread, then we will go to our work and leave them there. They will not be able to find the way back home and we will be rid of them."

"No," said the man. "I don't want to do that. How could I abandon my children in the forest? The wild animals will eat them."

"Oh, you fool!" exclaimed his wife. "If we don't do it all four of us will starve. Is that what you want?"

She would give him no peace until he gave in.

Hansel and Gretel were so hungry that they could not sleep and consequently they heard everything the woman said.

Gretel started crying and said, "Oh Hansel, what are we going to do?"

"Hush now, Gretel," said Hansel. "Don't worry, I will find a way to get us out of trouble."

When his parents were asleep, Hansel got up, put on his clothes and slipped outside.

The moon was full and bright, and the little stones which lay in front of the house sparkled

like silver pieces. Hansel bent down and filled his pockets with as many of the pebbles as he could carry.

Then he went back inside and whispered to Gretel, "Sleep in peace, little sister. I have a plan which will save us." Then he went back to bed.

Early in the morning, an hour before sunrise, the woman roused the two children, shaking them roughly.

"Wake up, you lazy children. We all have to go to the forest to gather wood," she snapped.

Then she gave each of them a little piece of bread and said, "This is your breakfast, but don't eat it too soon because you won't get any more food today."

Gretel put the two pieces of bread in her apron because Hansel's pockets were full of stones, then they set off together to the forest.

Before they reached the wood, Hansel stopped to look back at the house. He did this so often that his father became curious.

"Why do you keep stopping to look at the house?" he asked. "Watch out you don't trip over your own legs!"

"I'm looking at my white cat," replied Hansel. "He's sitting on the top of the roof and wants to say goodbye to me."

"Fool!" said the woman. "That is not your little white cat, it is only the rising sun that shines on the chimney."

But of course, Hansel had really been lagging behind so that he could lay a trail with the stones which he had hidden in his pockets. One by one he dropped the pebbles on the ground.

When they arrived in the middle of the forest, their father said, "Now you two gather some wood and I will make you a fire so that you will not get cold."

Hansel and Gretel together did as he said and soon they had made a pile of firewood as tall as a little hill.

Their father lit the fire and when the flames were burning high his wife said, "Children, sit close by the fire and rest. We will go further into the forest to chop trees. When we have finished we will come back for you."

Hansel and Gretel sat near the fire and at midday they both ate their little pieces of bread. All the time they could hear the sound of an axe, so they thought that their father was not far away. But the noise did not come from an axe at all – it was only a branch which their father had fastened to a tree, blowing backwards and forwards in the wind.

At last the children's eyes closed with exhaustion and they fell sound asleep.

When they finally awoke it was already dark.

Gretel began to cry and said, "How will we find our way out of the forest?"

"Wait until the moon has risen," answered
Hansel, hugging her, "then we will find our way
back."

As soon as the moon rose, Hansel took his little
sister by the hand and they followed the path of
little stones which glittered like silver pieces and
marked the way home.

It was almost daylight when they reached home.

They knocked at the door and, when the
woman opened it and saw it was Hansel and

Gretel, she said, "You naughty children, where have you been all night? We thought you were lost."

Their father was delighted to see them and welcomed them into the house. But it wasn't long before, once again, the children overheard the woman complaining to their father.

"We only have half a loaf of bread and after that is finished there is nothing left to eat. We have to get rid of the children. We will take them even further into the forest so that they cannot find their way back. There is no other solution."

Their father was heartbroken and thought it would be better to share the last piece of bread with the children instead of sending them away, but the woman did not want to hear any more about it and started to scold him until at last he gave in again.

When their parents were asleep, Hansel got up and went to gather stones as he had done before, but this time the door was locked and Hansel could not go outside.

Nevertheless, he comforted his little sister and said, "Don't worry, I will find a way to get us out of trouble."

Early in the morning the woman got the children out of bed and gave them each a little piece of bread, even smaller than the last time.

While they walked to the forest, Hansel kept stopping to drop crumbs on the ground, crumbled from the bread he had in his pocket.

"Hansel, why do you keep lagging behind?" said his father. "Hurry up!"

"I am looking at my pigeon that is sitting on the top of the roof and wants to say goodbye to me," replied Hansel.

"You fool!" exclaimed the woman. "That is not your pigeon, it is only the rising sun lighting up the chimney."

Hansel continued to secretly drop breadcrumbs along the path.

Deeper and deeper into the forest they were taken, where they had never been before in their lives.

As before, their father lit a big fire for them and the woman said, "Stay here by the fire. We are going into the forest to chop trees and in the evening, when we are finished, we will come to take you home again."

At midday Gretel shared her piece of bread with Hansel, who had crumbled his piece along the road, then they went to sleep. They did not awake until it was dark and no one came to fetch them. Hansel comforted his little sister by saying:

"Wait, Gretel, until the moon has risen, then we will be able to see the crumbs I have scattered.

They will show us the way home."

When the moon rose they got up, but they could not find any crumbs because the birds that lived in the forest had eaten them all.

"Never mind, we will find the way back ourselves," said Hansel.

But they could not find it. They walked the entire night, and even the next day from sunrise to sunset, without finding their way out of the forest.

They were very hungry for they had not had

anything to eat other than a few wild strawberries that they had found growing by the path. At last they were so tired that their legs could not carry them any longer, so they lay down under a tree and fell asleep.

Next day they tried again to find their way home, but still they only went deeper and deeper into the forest.

Near midday, they saw a beautiful bird, as white as snow, perched on a branch and singing so beautifully that the children almost forgot their hunger as they stopped to listen.

Then the bird spread its wings and flew away. The children followed the bird to a little house. When they came closer they saw with amazement that the little house was made of gingerbread and cakes, and the windows were made of brown sugar.

"This is just what we need," said Hansel. "We will make a good meal from it. I am going to start with the roof. Gretel, why don't you try some of the window?"

Hansel climbed on to the roof and broke off a piece, while Gretel began to lick the windows.

Suddenly, a soft voice came from inside:

"Nibble, nibble, mouse!
Who is nibbling at my little house?"

And the children answered:

"The wind, the wind,
Only the wind."

They carried on eating without another thought as they were still very hungry. Hansel, who liked the taste of the roof, tore down a large piece of it, and Gretel pushed out an entire window-pane, which she then began to nibble.

Suddenly the door opened and an old, bent woman came creeping out. Hansel and Gretel were so frightened that they dropped their sweets.

The old woman nodded her head and said, "My dear children, however did you get here? Come inside and stay with me in my house – you will enjoy it here."

She took both children by the hand and led them into the little house. There she gave them a delicious meal – milk and pancakes with sugar,

apples and nuts. Then she prepared two little beds
in which Hansel and Gretel were soon fast asleep,
thinking they were in heaven.

Now this old woman seemed very friendly, but
in reality she was a mean witch who caught and
ate little children. She had built her little house of
gingerbread to trap them, then she fed them until
they were fat enough to eat.

This witch didn't have very good eyesight, but
she had an excellent sense of smell. When she
smelled Hansel and Gretel approaching the house,

she laughed an evil cackle and cried, "They will not escape!"

The next morning she woke Hansel, grabbed him with her shrivelled hand and took him to a small stable where she locked him up behind a door with bars for a window. Then she went back to Gretel and shook her until she awoke.

"Get up, you lazy child," she cried. "Go and get me some water so that I can cook something nice for your brother. He is in the stable and has to be fattened up. As soon as he is fat enough, I will eat him."

Gretel began to weep, but all in vain. She was forced to do what the witch had ordered. The witch then prepared Hansel some of the best food, but to Gretel she gave only crab shells.

Every morning the old woman crept into the stable and cried, "Hansel, stretch out your finger, so I can feel if you have become fat."

But Hansel stretched out a little bone he had found on the floor and, because the witch was short-sighted, she thought it was his finger and was surprised that he was not getting any fatter.

Four weeks passed by in this way. Hansel remained thin and eventually her impatience got the better of her. One day she decided that she could not wait any longer.

"Hurry up, Gretel, bring me some water," she ordered the young girl. "Whether Hansel is fat or thin, I will kill him and cook him tomorrow."

Gretel wept and wept. "If the wild beasts in the forest had eaten us, we would at least have died together!" she sobbed.

"Spare me your whining," said the witch. "It will not help you in any way."

The following morning Gretel had to fill the big cooking pot with water and light the fire.

"First we will bake some bread," said the witch. "I have heated the oven and kneaded the dough."

She pushed poor Gretel towards the burning flames that came out of the oven.

"Creep inside to see whether it is warm enough, so that we can put the bread in."

Gretel guessed that once she was inside the witch would close the door and roast her to eat as well, so she scratched her head and pretended to look puzzled.

"I don't know how to get inside," she said.

"Oh you stupid goose!" said the witch. "The opening is big enough. You see, I even fit inside it myself."

She put her head into the oven door. Gretel immediately gave a great shove and pushed the old witch right inside the hot oven. Then she shut the iron door and fastened the bolt. That soon put an end to the evil witch!

Gretel ran quickly to Hansel, opened the stable door and cried, "Hansel, we are free! The old witch is dead!"

How they danced with joy and hugged each other. Then, as they had nothing to be afraid of any longer, they went through the entire house

where they found all sorts of precious pearls and stones.

Laughing, the two children gathered up as much treasure as they could carry. Hansel filled his pockets and Gretel filled her apron.

"Now, let's go quickly. I'm sure we will now be able to find our way out of this bewitched forest," said Hansel.

After they had walked through the forest for an hour or two the children arrived at a great river.

"We will not be able to get over to the other side," said Hansel. "I don't see a bridge or raft."

"There is not even a boat," agreed Gretel. "But look, there is a white duck. If I ask it kindly, perhaps it will help us to cross the river."

And she cried:

> "Little duck, little duck, do you see,
> Hansel and Gretel are waiting for thee?
> There's never a plank, or bridge in sight,
> Take us across on your back so white."

The duck swam towards them right away and Hansel seated himself on its back.

He wanted his sister to sit next to him.

"No," said Gretel. "Both of us will be too heavy for the duck. It will take us across, one by one."

When they were both safely on the other side of the river they started walking again. As they walked, the forest became more familiar and the children began to see things that they recognized.

At last they gave a glad cry as they saw the clearing where their own home was.

Then the children began to run; they burst into the house and flung their arms around their father's neck.

The man was overjoyed to see his children safe and sound. He had not known one happy hour since he had left them behind in the forest and his wife was now dead.

Gretel emptied her apron pocket and the pearls and precious stones rolled around the room. Hansel threw one handful of jewels after another out of his pocket.

At last all their worries were over. From that day on the family never knew a hungry day and they all lived together in perfect happiness.

The Little Match Girl

It was the last night of the year, New Year's Eve. and it was so terribly cold! It was snowing, and soon it would be dark.

Through the cold and the darkness, a poor little girl wandered in the street, with bare feet and no scarf for her head. She had, indeed, worn slippers when she left home, but they were not much use. They were very big slippers that her mother had worn before her. They were so big that the little girl had lost them rushing to cross the street in between two carts.

One of the slippers was nowhere to be found, and the other was taken by a boy who intended to use it as a cradle when he had children of his own.

The little girl wandered along in her bare feet which were blue with cold. She was carrying several matches in her old apron and was holding one bundle in her hand. It had been a bad day for her; no one had bought any matches and she had not earned a single penny. She was very hungry and very cold, and looked very frail. Poor little girl!

Lights were glittering from all the windows and there was a wonderful smell of roasting meat along the whole street. All the little girl could think of was that it was New Year's Eve. She sat down and tried to warm herself in a corner between two houses. She grew colder and colder, but she did not dare to go home for she would have to take back all the matches, but not one penny. Her father would beat her and, besides, it would be cold at home as well. They only lived in a little hut and the wind blew right through it, even though the biggest cracks had been stuffed with straw and rags.

Her little hands were almost dead with cold. A lighted match would at least do some good! Maybe she would dare to take just one out of the

bundle, strike it against the wall, and warm her fingers!

And so she took one. Whoosh! How it sparkled! How it burned! It was a gentle warm flame, just like a little candle when she held her hand around it. But what a strange light! It seemed to the little girl as if she were sitting in front of a huge iron stove with polished brass knobs and gleaming pots and pans. The fire was magnificent and gave out so much warmth! The child had just stretched her feet out to warm them, when the flame went out and the stove disappeared. She was sitting there with only a little burnt match-end in her hand.

The girl struck another match which burned and glowed, and where the light fell on the wall it became transparent like gauze. The child could see into a room where a table was covered with a white cloth and set with fine china. There was a roast goose, stuffed with prunes and apples, which filled the room with a delicious smell. What a surprise! Suddenly the goose jumped from its plate and rolled on the floor, straight to the poor girl, with the fork and knife still in its back.

Then the match went out and there was nothing

to see but the thick, cold wall.

She struck a third match. Immediately she found herself sitting under a magnificent Christmas tree. It was even bigger and more beautifully decorated than the one she had seen through the glass doors at the rich merchant's house last Christmas. A thousand candles were burning on the green branches, and it seemed as if all the colorful figures were smiling at her. The little girl held up both hands and the match went out. The Christmas candles rose higher and higher, and she then realized they were just stars. One of them fell and made a long streak of fire in the sky.

"Someone is dying," whispered the little girl, for her old grandmother, who was the only one who had ever been kind to her, but who had died, used to say to her: "If you see a falling star it means that a soul is going up to heaven."

She struck another match against the wall which made a great light. This time in the middle of that brightness she saw her grandmother. She looked so sweet and so shining.

"Oh Granny, take me with you," cried the girl. "When the match goes out, I know you won't be there any longer. You will disappear just like the iron stove, the roasted goose and the beautiful Christmas tree."

She suddenly struck the rest of the bundle because she wanted to keep her grandmother, and the matches shone so gloriously that it was brighter than daylight. Never before had her grandmother seemed so tall and so beautiful. She took the little girl in her arms and they both flew away in radiant joy, higher and higher until there was no more cold, no more hunger and no more suffering. They were in Paradise.

In the cold, early morning, the little girl was still sitting in the corner between the two houses. Her cheeks were red and she had a smile on her lips… She was dead, frozen to death on New Year's Eve.

New Year's morning rose over her little body sitting there with the matches, one bundle almost completely burnt up.

"She just wanted to keep herself warm!" someone said.

But no one knew what beautiful things she had seen, nor in what radiance she had entered the New Year with her old grandmother.

Puss in Boots

Once there was a miller who, when he died, had nothing to leave his children but his mill, his donkey and his cat. The property was soon divided, without involving a lawyer or a judge since their fees would have taken the whole meager inheritance. The eldest son had the mill, the second son had the donkey and the youngest had only the cat.

The third son was not happy with such a small inheritance.

"My brothers can earn an honest living by

working together," he said. "But as for me, once I have eaten the cat and made myself a scarf out of his skin, what shall I do?"

The cat overheard his speech and drew himself up in a dignified manner.

"Don't worry, my master. You only need to give me a drawstring bag, and have a pair of boots made for me so that I can go through thick under-growth, and you will see that you are not half as badly off as you thought."

Although the cat's master did not have much confidence in this promise, he decided he would try anything to escape being poor. And, after all, he had seen his cat perform cunning tricks in order to catch rats and mice.

When the cat was given what he had asked for, he put on the boots. Then he put some grain and lettuce in the bag, slung the bag over his shoulder and set off for a den where he knew there was a large number of rabbits. There he stretched out on the ground as if he were dead and then waited for some young innocent rabbit to go into his bag to eat the bait.

He had no sooner lain down, when his plan worked. A young rabbit was tempted into the bag, where the clever cat trapped it by immediately pulling the drawstrings. Very proud of his catch, he went to the palace to seek an audience with the king.

He was taken to His Majesty's room where he bowed deeply and said, "Majesty, here is a wild rabbit I am commanded to present to you in the name of the Marquis de Carabas." (This was the name he had made up for his master.)

"Tell your master that I am very pleased and that I thank him," replied the king.

A few days later the cat hid in a wheat field and set his trap again. When two partridges wandered into the bag he pulled the strings and caught them both. Then he went to the king, as he had done with the wild rabbit. The king accepted the two partridges with great pleasure and gave the cat something to drink.

The cat continued in this way for two or three months, visiting the king from time to time to take him game supposedly from his master's hunting.

One day when he heard that the king was going for a drive along the river bank with his daughter, the most beautiful princess in the world, the cat said to his master, "If you would follow my

53

advice, your fortune is made. You only have to bathe in the river at the place I will show you and then let me do the rest."

The young man did what his cat advised him, although he wondered what good it would do him.

While he was bathing, the king passed by and the cat started to shout at the top of his voice, "Help! Help! My master, the Marquis de Carabas is drowning here!"

When the king heard this cry he put his head out of the carriage window and recognized the cat who had brought him game so many times. He ordered his guards to rescue the Marquis.

While the poor young man was being pulled out of the river, the cat approached the carriage and told the king that some wicked thieves had stolen his master's clothes. (The cat had, in fact, hidden them under a big stone!) The king immediately ordered his Master of the Wardrobe to pick out one of his most beautiful suits for the Marquis de Carabas.

The king paid the young man a lot of attention, and the beautiful clothes that were given to him emphasized his handsome face and figure. The

king's daughter admired him a great deal; indeed, it wasn't long before she was completely in love with him. The king invited the marquis to get into the carriage to join them for the rest of the trip.

The cat was delighted to see that his plan had started to work, but there was still a great deal to do. He ran on ahead and soon came across some farmers cutting hay in a meadow.

"Listen farmers," he said, "if you do not tell the king that the field you are working in belongs to the Marquis de Carabas, you will all be chopped up as fine as meat for hamburgers.

Sure enough, when the king arrived he asked the farmers whose field they were working on.

"It belongs to the Marquis de Carabas," they all replied.

"You have a considerable inheritance there," said the king to the Marquis de Carabas.

"As you see, Majesty, it is a meadow which provides for an abundant crop every single year," answered the young man, although he had been truly astonished by their words.

The ingenious cat, still walking ahead, next encountered some harvesters, and told them, "Listen harvesters, if you do not say that all this

wheat belongs to the Marquis de Carabas you will be ground up as fine as meat for hamburgers."

The king, who passed by a moment later, asked to whom all the wheat belonged.

"It belongs to the Marquis de Carabas," answered the harvesters, and the king was even more delighted with the young man.

The cat, who walked well ahead of the carriage, kept on saying the same thing to everyone he encountered, and the king was astonished to see the immense wealth of the Marquis de Carabas.

Finally the artful cat arrived at a beautiful castle belonging to an ogre; indeed, all the land the king had been driving through was part of the estate of this castle. The cat knew this and asked to speak to the ogre. The ogre received him as courteously as an ogre can, and asked him to sit down.

"I have been informed," said the cat, "that you possess the gift of being able to change yourself into all sorts of animals; that you could transform yourself, for example, into a lion or an elephant?"

"That is true," answered the ogre brusquely, "and just to show you, I will change into a lion."

The cat was so terrified to see a lion before him that he jumped for the nearest rafter to reach the

59

safety of the roof, but the boots he was wearing made it difficult and dangerous.

When the ogre had changed back again, he came down and licked his ruffled fur.

"I have also been informed," continued the cat, "that you also have the power to take the form of smaller animals. For example, that you can change yourself into a rat or a mouse. I find this almost impossible to believe."

"Impossible? Wait and see!" exclaimed the ogre. At once he changed himself into a mouse and started running across the floor.

The cat no sooner saw the mouse, than he pounced, caught and ate it!

In the meantime, the king had arrived at the ogre's castle and wanted to call on the owner. Hearing the sound of the carriage rumbling across the drawbridge, the cat ran towards it and said to the king, "Your Majesty, welcome to the castle of the Marquis de Carabas."

"What! Monsieur le Marquis!" cried the king. "The castle also belongs to you?! I have never seen anything more beautiful than this courtyard and all the buildings around it. Let us see inside, please."

The young man gave the princess his hand and followed the king into a large room where a magnificent meal was laid out. The ogre had had this meal prepared for his friends who should have been visiting him that day, but who had not dared to approach the castle knowing the king was there.

Both the king and his daughter were quite charmed by the excellent qualities of the Marquis de Carabas. Having also seen all the wealth the marquis possessed, the king at last said to him, "I see no reason why, if you agree, you should not be my son-in-law, Monsieur le Marquis."

The Marquis, bowing low, accepted the honor the king did him; and that very day he married the princess.

The clever cat was given the title 'Great Lord' and never again ran after mice, except for fun!

Beauty and the Beast

Once upon a time there was a rich merchant. He had six children – three boys and three girls.

His daughters were very beautiful, but the youngest was admired the most. She was called Beauty because the name suited her, which made her sisters green with envy. And if this were not enough, she was also more intelligent than her sisters.

One day the merchant lost everything he owned, except for a little cottage far away from the city. In tears he told his children that they would have to move to the cottage and that, from now on, they would have to make a living by farming.

And so they moved into the cottage, and the merchant and his three sons became farmers and learned to work the land.

Each morning Beauty would wake up at four o'clock and hurry to clean the house and make breakfast for the family. When she had finished the housework she spent her time reading, playing the harpsichord or singing.

In contrast, her two sisters were always bored. They didn't wake until ten o'clock in the morning; then they would go for long walks and pass their time talking about all the friends and beautiful clothes they'd once had. They looked with scorn and jealousy on Beauty's simple pleasures.

"Look at our youngest sister," they said to each other. "She is so stupid that she is happy in her misery."

When they had been in the cottage for about a year the merchant received a letter telling him of a ship which would make his fortune. In haste he made ready to travel on the long journey to the port.

The good news made the two elder sisters excited. When their father was ready to leave they danced around him and begged him to bring them new dresses and all kinds of presents. Beauty, however, said nothing.

"Don't you want me to buy you anything?" asked her father.

"There is nothing I really need," she said, "but, since you are so kind as to ask, would you please bring me back a rose if you should see one on your travels? There are no bushes to be found in these parts and they are the one thing that I have truly missed since we have been here."

And so their father left, but when he arrived at the port he found that the ship's cargo was worthless and he had to return home just as poor as he had been before.

Sadly he started the long journey back, disappointed that he could not even afford one present for his children.

He was only about thirty miles from home when disaster struck once more. While riding through a vast forest he somehow missed his way and became lost. It began to snow heavily and the wind was so strong that he was twice thrown from his horse. When darkness came he was sure he would starve of hunger or cold, or that he would be eaten by the howling wolves.

Suddenly he saw a light at the end of a long tree-lined path. It seemed quite far away but just the thought of shelter gave the merchant a little strength.

He walked towards it and saw that the light came from a brightly lit palace. Astonished, he passed through the gateway; the courtyard was quite empty.

His horse, which followed him, saw an empty stable and went inside. The cold, starving animal found some hay and oats which it started to eat greedily, while the merchant walked to the house.

Still he found no one, but when he entered a large hall, there he found a welcoming fire blazing in the fireplace and a table full of food, set for just one person.

The merchant was soaked to the skin so he went to the fireplace to dry himself off.

"The master of the house will forgive me for making myself at home," he thought. "He will probably arrive soon and I can explain."

He waited for quite a long time, but when still no one had arrived by eleven o'clock he could no longer resist his hunger and helped himself to a chicken which he ate in two bites. Then he drank a couple of glasses of wine which made him very sleepy.

He left the hall and passed through several huge corridors, all magnificently decorated. At the end of one he found a bedroom in which there was a comfortable bed. The sight of it was too much for the tired man; without thinking further, he threw himself into it and fell fast asleep.

The merchant slept well and did not wake up until ten o'clock the next morning. When he got up and looked for his clothes he was very surprised to find that they had been replaced by brand-new ones.

After a magnificent breakfast he went outside to find his horse.

On the way he walked under a rose-covered archway and, remembering Beauty's request, he picked a branch on which there grew several roses.

"At least one of my dear children will have a gift," he smiled to himself.

Suddenly he heard a terrible noise and saw a beast coming towards him, a monster so horrible that he almost fainted in terror.

"You ungrateful wretch," roared the Beast. "I saved your life by letting you into my palace, and you reward me by stealing my roses which I love more than anything in the world. Now you will die!"

The merchant fell to his knees and begged the Beast not to harm him.

"Forgive me, Sir, I did not think you would be offended if I picked a rose for one of my daughters

who wanted one so badly."

"Don't call me Sir. I am known as the Beast," answered the creature. "I prefer it that people say what they think, so don't think your flattery will change anything.

"However, I will forgive you on condition that one of your daughters comes here willingly to die in your place. If your daughters refuse to die for you, you must return to me in three months and receive your punishment."

The man had no intention of sacrificing one of his daughters to the evil monster, but he said to himself, "At least I will have the chance to embrace them one more time before I die."

So he promised that he would return and, fetching his horse, he left the palace.

A few hours later the man arrived home, tired and sad.

His children ran towards him with open arms, but the merchant looked at them with tears in his eyes. In his hand he held the branch of roses he brought for Beauty.

He gave it to her and said, "Take these roses; your unhappy father has indeed paid a great price for them."

Then he told his family all about the worthless ship, the magical palace and the misfortune that had befallen him.

After hearing his story, his two older daughters started to cry.

But Beauty said, "There is no need for our father to die. I will willingly offer myself to the Beast in his place."

"No, my sister," said her three brothers. "We will track down the monster and kill him first. Surely all three of us can defeat him."

"My children," said the merchant, "this Beast is too powerful even for you. Besides, the Beast saved my life, although he now intends to take it. I gave my word: I am old and will not regret losing the last few years of my life, thanks to you, my dear children."

"I assure you, my father, that you will not go to the palace without me," said Beauty. "You can't stop me from following you. I would rather be eaten by this monster than die of a broken heart from losing you."

Her father and brothers begged and pleaded with her, but there was nothing they could say to make her change her mind.

The two elder daughters rubbed their eyes with an onion and pretended to cry when Beauty left with her father. Her brothers and her father also wept, but Beauty didn't cry at all because she did not want to make her family even more miserable.

They rode the horse to the palace and, as darkness fell, found it as brightly lit as before.

The horse found shelter in the stable and the man entered the large hall with his daughter, where they found a table magnificently laid out and set for two.

Beauty thought to herself, "The Beast wants to

fatten me up before he eats me."

After dinner they heard a great roaring. Beauty could hardly stop herself from fainting in terror when she saw the horrible monster, but she tried to control her fear and, when the Beast asked her if she had come of her own choice, she told him with a trembling voice that she had.

"You are very kind," said the Beast, "and I am very grateful that you decided to come."

He then turned to the man and said to him, "Say goodbye to your daughter. You will leave here tomorrow morning and never come back. Now, goodnight, Beauty!"

"Goodnight, Beast," she answered, and the monster disappeared.

That night, while she slept, Beauty dreamed of a fairy who told her, "I like and admire your kind heart, Beauty. The good deed you have done will be rewarded."

When Beauty woke up she told her father of her dream. Although this comforted him a little, it did not stop him from weeping bitterly when he had to leave his daughter.

When he had gone, Beauty sat down in the large hall and began to weep herself, thinking that the

Beast must surely eat her that night. Then, pulling herself together, she decided to explore.

She was very surprised when she came to a door with a sign that read, 'Beauty's Room'. She opened it and was impressed by what she saw: a large library, a harpsichord and several books about music.

On a shelf was a book inscribed in gold letters, 'Wish, command: *here you are the queen and the mistress*'.

"Alas!" she sighed. "I only wish I could see my poor father to know what he is doing at this very moment."

To her surprise, in the mirror she saw a vision of her father arriving home, looking very sad. All too soon the vision disappeared, but Beauty was no longer scared because she believed the Beast didn't mean to eat her after all.

At noon she found the table set with food for her. During the meal she could hear beautiful music, although she never saw anyone playing.

In the afternoon Beauty walked in the palace gardens. She felt quite safe, but that evening, as she sat at the table, she heard the noise of the Beast arriving and could not help shivering.

"Beauty, would you mind if I watched you have your dinner?" he asked.

"You are the master," answered Beauty trembling.

"Yes, but you are the only mistress here," assured the Beast. "You only have to tell me if I bore you and I will leave at once. Tell me, don't you think I am very ugly?"

"I admit that is true because I can't lie," said Beauty. "But I think that you are very kind."

"But that doesn't change my dreadful ugliness," said the monster." I know very well that I am just a beast."

"One is only a beast if one thinks it," Beauty assured him, kindly. "Only fools are not aware of that."

"Enjoy your meal, Beauty," said the monster. "Everything in this house is yours and I would be sad if you were unhappy."

"You are very kind," said Beauty, "and I appreciate your generosity."

"Oh yes, Beauty!" answered the Beast. "I have a good heart, but I am still a monster."

Beauty enjoyed her meal. She was no longer afraid of the monster, but she was very shocked when he suddenly said, "Beauty, will you marry me?"

She waited a moment before answering. She feared that if she refused the monster would be angry.

At last she told him with a trembling voice, "No, Beast."

The poor monster wanted to sigh, but instead he made a dreadful hissing noise that echoed through the whole palace.

Then he sadly said, "Goodnight Beauty."

He left the room, sadly looking over his shoulder before he closed the door.

Beauty felt sorry for the poor Beast.

"Alas!" she said. "He is so kind, but I could never love a Beast."

Beauty spent three very happy months in the palace. Every evening the Beast would visit her and talk to her while she had dinner.

Every day, Beauty discovered new virtues in the monster and she became quite fond of him.

Just one thing troubled her; at night, before the monster went to bed he always asked her if she would become his wife, and every time he seemed to be overcome with pain when she refused.

One day she said to him, "You make me sad, Beast. I will always be your friend, but I could never marry you."

"If that is how it has to be," said the Beast, "I deserve what I get. I know very well I am horrible to look at. Nevertheless, promise me that you will never leave me."

These words embarrassed Beauty. She was missing her father a great deal and, although she could see a vision of him in the mirror any time she liked, she dearly wished to be able to speak to him

again and assure him that she was alive and well. She could also see how much he was missing her.

"I could promise never to leave you, but I would so much like to see my father once more. I would die of a broken heart if you were to refuse me this wish," said Beauty.

"I would rather die myself, than to make you unhappy," replied the monster. "But if I send you to your father you will stay there, and your poor Beast will die of heartbreak."

"No," answered Beauty. "I promise that I will return within a week. Your mirror has shown me that my sisters have married and that my brothers are now soldiers. My father is all alone – allow me to visit him for a week."

"You will be there tomorrow morning," said the Beast, giving her a jewelled ring. "Remember your promise. When you want to return you only have to put this magic ring on a table and go to sleep. Farewell, Beauty."

Having said this the Beast sighed as usual and Beauty went sadly to sleep, feeling guilty that she had hurt his feelings.

When she woke up the next morning she was in her father's house. He was beside himself with joy when he saw his sweet daughter again, and they embraced each other for a very long time.

When Beauty's sisters heard the news they rushed to the house with their husbands. They were furious when they saw her dressed like a princess and more beautiful than ever.

She was very sweet to them, but nothing could stop them from being jealous.

The two girls went to the garden to grumble together.

"Listen my sister," said the eldest. "I have an

idea. Let's try to make her stay here longer than a week. Her stupid Beast will be angry because she didn't keep her promise and maybe he will tear her to shreds."

"You are right, my sister," answered the other. "Let us be very sweet to her."

When a week had passed the two sisters begged so prettily for Beauty to stay that she promised to remain one more week.

Yet Beauty blamed herself for the grief she must be causing the poor Beast and, indeed, she even found that she missed his company.

The tenth night she spent at her father's house, she dreamt that she was in the palace garden. She saw the Beast stretched out on the grass – he was dying of a broken heart because she had not returned to him.

Beauty woke up in shock and began to weep.

"How could I break a Beast's heart who is so sweet to me!" she cried. "Is it his fault that he is so ugly, and has no hope? He is kind, and that is more important than anything else. I could never forgive myself if he died for my ingratitude."

So Beauty got up, put her magic ring on the table, and went back to sleep.

When she woke up the next morning she was delighted to find that she was back in the Beast's palace.

She dressed herself quickly, then spent all that day waiting for the Beast to arrive. She waited and waited, until the clock struck nine, but the Beast did not appear.

Beauty then feared the worst. She ran through the palace, searching desperately for the Beast. After she'd looked everywhere, she suddenly remembered her dream and ran out to the garden where she had seen him lying.

There she found the Beast unconscious on the ground and she thought he was dead.

She threw herself on him without a thought for his ugliness and felt his heart still beating, although only just. She took some water from the pond and threw it on his face.

At last the Beast opened his eyes and said, "You did not keep your promise, Beauty! But now I will die happily because I have had the chance to see you one more time."

Once more he closed his eyes and Beauty stroked his forehead.

"No, my dear Beast, you will not die," she said.

"You have put virtue above beauty, and you deserve this prince who has such qualities himself. You will become a great queen and I have no fear that you will rule wisely and well."

Then the fairy turned to Beauty's two sisters.

"I know your evil hearts," she said. "You will become two stone statues that will stand at your sister's palace gate. All you will do each day is to witness her happiness, and there you will stay until the moment you admit your mistakes. However, I am afraid that you may well remain statues for a very long time."

That very day the Prince, who had been the Beast, married Beauty. She lived with him in the palace in perfect happiness forever after because, after all, their love was a tale of honest virtue.

The Emperor's New Clothes

Many years ago there was a grand emperor who was so fond of new clothes that he spent all his money on them. Every hour of the day he changed his clothes.

Whether he was inspecting his soldiers, going to the theater or taking a walk, the real reason he went was to show off his new clothes.

The capital was a very lively city thanks to the many tourists who visited it. One day two thieves arrived who, knowing of the emperor's fondness for clothes, spread the story that they were weavers and that they knew how to weave the most magnificent cloth in the world. Not only were the colors and the patterns outstandingly beautiful, but the clothes made from this cloth were magic. They were invisible to every person who did not do his job properly or to anyone who was stupid.

"Such clothes are beyond price," thought the emperor. "If I had a suit of this cloth I would know which men in my government are not fit for their jobs, and I would be able to pick out the wise men from the fools. Yes, I certainly must have this cloth."

He gave the thieves a large sum of money and asked them to start their work immediately.

They set up two looms and acted as if they were weaving, although there was nothing at all to be seen. They constantly asked for the finest silk yarn and gold thread; but really they hid everything in their own bags and just pretended to work, long into the night, on the empty looms.

"I would like to know how far they have got with my cloth," thought the emperor a few days later. But he was a bit afraid to go himself when he remembered that anyone who was stupid or no

He nodded in satisfaction while he looked at the loom. He did not dare to tell the truth. All the people he had taken with him stared hard as well, one after the other. Although they could not see anything, they repeated after the emperor, "It is magnificent! It is charming! It is delightful!"

Everyone appeared happy with the result and the emperor commanded that there was to be a procession the next day, at which he would wear his new suit.

Then the two crooks were given knighthoods and received the title of Gentlemen Weavers.

That night they sat up working in the light of sixteen candles. They pretended to take the cloth from the loom; they cut into the air with a huge pair of scissors and sewed with a needle that had no thread in it. Finally they declared with a great flourish that the suit was finished.

Together with his courtiers, the emperor went to see the finished clothes.

The two thieves both stood with their arms in the air as if they were holding up something, and said, "Here are the trousers, Your Majesty. Here is the jacket, here is the cloak. They are as light as a feather, so light that it may seem as if you are not wearing anything, but that is one of the important qualities of this cloth."

"Yes, of course," answered the courtiers.

But they did not see anything; after all, there was nothing to see!

"Would Your Highness be graciously pleased to take off your clothes?" asked the thieves. "Then you can try on the new ones in front of the big mirror."

The emperor took his clothes off and the thieves pretended to dress him. He turned round and round in front of the mirror.

"Good gracious! How well it suits His Majesty! What a perfect fit!" exclaimed all the courtiers. "What style! What colours! What a wonderful suit!"

Then the chief master of ceremonies entered.

"The canopy which is to be carried over Your Majesty in the procession is waiting outside," he said.

"Excellent! I am ready," answered the emperor. "I think I look quite good in these clothes."

And he twirled in front of the mirror one more time to look at the splendid suit.

The attendants, who had to carry the cloak's long train, pretended to pick it up from the ground; then they held their hands as if they were holding the train because they did not want anyone to think that they could not see it.

The emperor walked very proudly in the procession under his beautiful canopy, and all the people in the street and at the windows cried, "What a splendid costume! How gracious the train is! What a perfect fit!"

Nobody would let anyone else think that he could not see anything. Never had the emperor's clothes been so admired before.

Then the door opened once again. The little man appeared and said, "What will you give me if I spin this straw into gold?"

"The ring that I wear on my finger," answered the young girl.

The little man took the ring, sat himself down behind the spinning wheel, and by the next morning he had spun all the straw into sparkling gold.

The king was delighted at the sight of all this gold, but he still wasn't satisfied. He took the miller's daughter to another room full of straw, even larger than the first two, and commanded, "You will spin all this straw for me tonight, and if you succeed you will become my wife."

"Although she is only a miller's daughter," he thought, "I couldn't find a richer wife!"

When the young girl was alone, the little man arrived again and said, "What will you give me this time if I spin the straw into gold?"

"I don't have anything more to give," answered the young girl.

"Well, promise me your first child if you become queen," said the little man.

"That's never likely to happen!" thought the miller's daughter.

Still, she promised the little man his wish and again he spun all the straw into gold.

When the king arrived the next morning and saw all the gold he prepared the wedding and the pretty miller's daughter became queen, much to her surprise.

One year later, when she had forgotten all about the little man, she gave birth to a beautiful child.

Then one day he suddenly walked into her room and said, "Well, give me what you have promised."

The queen was terrified and offered the little man all the treasures of the kingdom not to take her child.

But the little man answered, "No, I have no need of treasure. You must keep your promise."

Then the queen started to moan and weep. The little man felt sorry for her, and he said, "I will give you three days. If within that time you discover my name, I will let you keep your child."

Throughout the whole night the queen thought about all the names she had ever heard, and she sent a messenger through the country to find out every name that existed.

When the little man arrived the next day she

started with Caspar, Melchior, Balthazar, and said
one name after another until she knew no more.

Every time the little man said, "That is not my
name."

The next day she had inquiries made throughout the entire neighborhood for the name of every
single person, and she repeated the strangest and
the rarest names to the little man.

"Isn't your name Cowribs, or Leg-of-Mutton,
or Spiderlegs?" she said.

But still he answered, "That is not my name."

The third day the messenger came back and said he was not able to find any new names.

"However," he said, "when I arrived at a huge mountain at the corner of a forest where the foxes and the hares say goodnight to each other, I saw a fire burning in front of a little house. A very strange little man was dancing around this fire. He was hopping on one leg and singing:

"Today I bake. Tomorrow I brew beer.
The day after tomorrow I will bring the
queen's child here.
How lucky I am that nobody knows
That Rumpelstiltskin is my name."

You can imagine how delighted the queen was when she heard that!

Soon afterwards, the little man entered and asked her, "What is my name?"

She answered, "Is your name Harry?"

"No."

"Is your name Bert?"

"No."

Then the queen laughed and said, "Is your name, by any chance … Rumpelstiltskin?"

fat rats in it. The fairy godmother chose the one with the finest whiskers. When she touched it with her magic wand, it changed into a coachman with the most handsome moustache in the world!

Then she said to Cinderella, "Go and look behind the watering-can. You will find six lizards there. Bring them to me."

Cinderella had no sooner brought them to her fairy godmother than she changed them into foot-men. They stepped up behind the carriage with their brightly-patterned uniforms and hung on as if they had never done anything else in their lives.

Then the fairy godmother said, "Well, now you can go to the ball in style. Aren't you delighted?"

"Yes, but how can I possibly go to the ball in these wretched clothes?" replied the girl.

Just one touch of the magic wand changed Cinderella's rags into a dress of gold and silver material, embroidered with precious stones. Finally the fairy godmother gave her a pair of glass slippers.

All dressed up, Cinderella got into the carriage. Her fairy godmother warned her to be home by midnight for the spell would break at the twelfth chime of the clock.

The girl promised her fairy godmother that she would and drove off.

The king's son had been told that an unknown princess was about to arrive at the ball, so he ran outside to welcome her. He helped Cinderella down from the carriage and led her into the ballroom.

As soon as everyone saw her they were awestruck. The dancing ceased and the fiddlers stopped playing as they all admired her perfect beauty.

Even the king himself, although he was an old man, could not keep his eyes off her, and he whispered to the queen that he had not seen such a beautiful young lady for a long time. The queen agreed with him, for truly the beautiful stranger outshone every other person in the room.

All the women studied her hairstyle and dress closely, wondering what far-off country could produce such elegant gowns in such magnificent materials. They were determined to remember every last detail so that they would be able to copy them next time there was a grand occasion.

The prince seated Cinderella in the best place and paid her many compliments. Then, later he led her on to the dance floor. She danced so gracefully that everyone admired her even more.

After the first round of dances there was a fine banquet, but the prince could not eat anything because he was too absorbed with the lovely stranger.

Cinderella sat next to the sisters and gave them all her attention, offering them oranges and lemons which the prince had given her. They were extremely surprised, but they did not recognize her at all.

Then the dancing started again. All the young men wanted to dance with the lovely girl, but the prince didn't give anyone a chance. Cinderella danced every dance with the prince, and when they rested he stayed at her side, making sure that she wanted for nothing.

Cinderella had never been happier in her life. Indeed, she was so absorbed with the handsome young man and his attention that she quite forgot her fairy godmother's warning.

Then the palace clock began to chime.

At the first stroke of midnight Cinderella realized her mistake and sprang to her feet, fleeing the ballroom.

The prince followed, but he could not catch her. However, in her hurry she dropped one of her dainty glass slippers. Still, the young girl ran and ran, not stopping to pick it up or even to look behind her.

Cinderella arrived home exhausted, without a carriage or her footmen, and dressed in her old clothes. Nothing remained of her splendor but the other glass slipper.

The prince asked the guards at the palace door if they had seen the princess leave. They said they had not seen anyone go out but a young girl dressed in rags, who looked more like a farmer's daughter than a lady.

When the sisters came home a little later on, Cinderella asked them if they'd enjoyed the ball. Excitedly they told her about the beautiful stranger who'd captivated the prince, and how she had run off suddenly into the night, leaving one slipper on the palace steps.

They told her that the prince had picked up the fallen glass slipper and had gazed at it for the rest of the evening. He had definitely fallen head over heels in love with the beautiful stranger, even though he didn't know who she was.

The sisters were telling the truth, for a few days later the king's son publicly announced that he would marry the girl whose foot would fit perfectly into the slipper.

But although all the princesses, then all the duchesses, and then all the rest of the court ladies in the land tried it on, not one could fit the delicate shoe.

The slipper was eventually brought to the two sisters, who squeezed and pushed, and pushed and squeezed, and tried with all their might to fit a foot into it, but all in vain.

Then Cinderella smiled and said, "I would like to try the slipper and see if it fits me!"

The sisters laughed and made fun of her, but the courtier had been given orders to let all the girls in the land try on the slipper. So he sat Cinderella down and, to everyone's surprise, the slipper fitted perfectly!

The two sisters were astonished, but not half as astonished as they were when Cinderella took the other glass slipper from her pocket and put it on.

At this moment the fairy godmother appeared and tapped Cinderella's clothes with her magic wand. At once the rags changed into a dress even more beautiful than the ones she had worn before.

Then the sisters recognized her as the kind lady they had met at the ball. They dropped to their knees and begged her to forgive them for all the suffering they had caused her.

Cinderella embraced them and said that she forgave them with all her heart.

Then she was taken to the prince in her splendid dress. He thought she was more beautiful than ever and, a few day later, he married her.

And, of course, you don't need me to tell you that they then lived happily ever after!

Reynard
and the
Fishermen

It was winter and Reynard the Fox had no more food in his store. Driven by starvation, he roamed near the villages without fearing the inhabitants. He hid under a hedge at the side of the main road, waiting for something exciting to happen.

Soon a little cart came along the road. In it were two fishermen who wanted to do business in the city. They had a huge catch of fresh herrings to sell, for the north wind had been blowing the

whole week and the fish were plentiful.

They also had baskets filled to the brim with fish, large and small, from the lakes and from the rivers: pike, eel, carp, trout and salmon.

Reynard got very excited at the sight and the smell of the fish cart and decided that this was his chance. So he stretched himself out in the middle of the road as if he were dead. He put his feet in the air, closed his eyes and held his breath.

One of the fishermen noticed him and said to his partner, "Let's pick up that fox. That's a good skin, easily gained!"

They approached Reynard cautiously, touched him and then turned him over, certain that he was dead. Then they estimated the value of his skin.

"We will sell it for three silver pieces," said one.

"No, we will easily get four silver pieces for it," said the other. "Maybe more – look how white the throat is!"

They threw Reynard into the back of the cart and continued on their way, talking cheerfully.

Reynard heard them talking and had a good laugh to himself at the bottom of the cart.

He lay flat on his stomach on top of the baskets, and, with his sharp teeth, he nibbled at a juicy

walked into a most amazing cave. There was enough light inside to see a collection of fabulous treasures – silk material, rich fabrics, carpets and, above all, bags overflowing with gold and silver. It was obviously the secret hide-out of a group of robbers.

After Ali Baba had recovered from his astonishment, he gathered as much gold as his three donkeys could carry and closed the cave with the magic words.

When he arrived home, he emptied his bags in front of his wife, who was dazzled by the gold. He then told her all about his adventure.

"We are rich!" she cried, dancing and clapping her hands. "But how much exactly do we have?"

"Enough to live in peace for the rest of our days," answered Ali Baba.

"I want to be sure. We must count it!" his wife demanded.

Ali Baba did not see any reason for this, but he did not want to upset his wife so he let her have her way. She immediately went to Cassim to ask him for a measuring cup.

Cassim's wife opened the door.

"A measuring cup?" she asked, astonished.

"Yes, the biggest one you have!" replied Ali Baba's wife.

Cassim's wife lent her the cup, but she secretly stuck some candle-wax on the bottom because she wanted to know what there was to measure at a poor woodcutter's house.

When Ali Baba's wife returned home she began to scoop up the gold with the cup. She filled it

As ill luck would have it, the thieves arrived at the cave. When they opened the magic door Cassim took the chance to escape. He was caught immediately by the thieves who killed him on the spot and cut him up into four pieces.

The next day Ali Baba came to the rock in search of his brother. To his horror he discovered his brother's remains. Weeping with shock and grief, he put the four pieces that were left of his brother on the donkeys and returned home to Cassim's widow to tell her the dreadful news.

Now, Cassim had a very clever servant whose name was Morgiane.

"Morgiane, we will have to cover up the true reason for Cassim's death!" said Ali Baba.

"Don't worry, I know how to handle that!" she replied.

The next day the servant went several times to the chemist, pretending that her master had fallen ill. Each time she asked for stronger and stronger medicines, saying that he was going from bad to worse. The following day, no one was surprised, therefore, to hear that Cassim had died.

Also in the city lived a very old, wise garment-maker called Baba Moustafa. Morgiane asked him

to come to her in secret, bringing the tools of his trade. Baba Moustafa, who was suspicious, did not agree to do so unless he was given a large sum of money. He was then blindfolded and led into Cassim's room.

There Morgiane took off the blindfold and asked him to sew her poor master's body back together. Baba Moustafa did so and, after he was finished, he was blindfolded again and taken home. In this way Cassim had a dignified funeral and no one was the least suspicious.

Ali Baba inherited his brother's house. As he liked that house better than his own, he moved in with his wife and they lived together with Cassim's widow and Morgiane the servant.

In the meantime, the forty thieves had not forgotten the intruder in their cave.

"Someone else knows our secret!" said the leader. "The pile of gold is smaller. Who will go into the city to see what can be found out?"

One of the thieves volunteered and left early the next morning in disguise. He soon found Baba Moustafa's shop in which the old wise man was busy with his work.

"Good man!" the thief said to the old man.

"How can you still see so clearly at your age?"

"Eh? I can see that you are not from around here!" said Baba Moustafa. "My eyes are the best in the city. Why, not long ago I sewed a dead man back together in a room much darker than this!"

"Go on... Where was that?" asked the thief.

"I don't know. I was taken there blindfolded," replied Baba Moustafa.

The thief held out a couple of gold pieces. "Take me there!"

"I told you, I was blindfolded!" said Baba Moustafa.

"Try to remember in which direction you were led!" pressed the thief.

Baba Moustafa accepted the challenge and, as he had a good memory, they soon arrived in front of Cassim's house, which was now Ali Baba's.

The thief thanked Baba Moustafa, then he secretly made a cross with chalk on the door and went back into the forest.

Shortly afterwards, Morgiane discovered the mark. She assumed that this mark was not a good sign so she took a piece of chalk of the same colour and drew crosses on all the other doors in the neighborhood.

That same night, the forty thieves sneaked into the city. They looked for the door marked with a cross, intending to kill the people who lived there. But when they found that every door had a cross they left in great anger.

The following day the leader decided to take things into his own hands. He too found Baba Moustafa, who led him to Ali Baba's house. The leader examined it closely and very soon he had an idea.

When he got back to the forest he sent his men to buy some mules and forty leather oil jars.

When everything had been bought the leader filled one of the jars with oil, leaving the others empty. Then he ordered all his men into the empty jars which he then sealed, leaving just a little air-hole in each lid.

That night he drove his strange convoy into the city. Ali Baba was enjoying the cool, night air when the leader of the thieves stopped outside, pretending that he was an oil merchant bound for market the following day. He said that he had come a long distance and was very tired.

Ali Baba did not recognize him at all.

"You are welcome here," Ali Baba said. "Come into my house and spend the night!"

The fake merchant put his jars in the courtyard under the window of the room where he would be staying. While Ali Baba was out of earshot the leader went to each jar and gave his orders.

"Can you hear me? When I throw little stones out of my window, split the vases from top to bottom with your knives and get out! I will then tell you what to do."

He went to bed early, keeping all his clothes on, ready for action.

Meanwhile, Morgiane was working in the kitchen when her oil lamp suddenly went out.

"Oh! What a time to run out of oil!" she cried.

"Well, go into the courtyard," said Abdalla, another servant. "There is plenty of oil as long as the merchant is here!"

So Morgiane took a jug and went outside. When she approached the first jar, she heard, "Hey! Is it time?"

That voice certainly came from the jar!

Morgiane, who was a quick thinker, realized the danger immediately and answered in a whisper, "Not yet, but soon!"

She went to the other jars, hearing the same question and giving the same answer, until she found the oil jar.

First she lit her lamp again, then she poured the oil from the last jar into a large copper pan which she put on the stove until it boiled. Then she poured boiling oil into each jar, killing all the thieves quickly and quietly.

Later, when the leader of the thieves threw the little stones out of his window, he was angry that there was no response. He went outside to wake up the thieves, but when he smelled the hot oil and leather he thought it wiser to leave quickly!

Next morning, when Ali Baba came back from the bath house, he was surprised to see the jars still in his courtyard.

Morgiane told him to open one of them and when he saw what was in it he jumped back in fright. Then the servant told him about how she had rescued him and his family.

Ali Baba realized that the men in the jars must be the thieves from the cave with the magic door.

As a reward he gave Morgiane her freedom.

He buried the bodies, sold the mules and carefully hid the weapons and the leather jars.

However, although the leader of the thieves had run off, he was not that far away. He longed to take his revenge on the man who had invaded his hoard and destroyed his gang.

In a little while he returned to the city, rented a shop and became a cloth merchant, calling himself Cogia Houssain. He made it his business to become very friendly with Ali Baba's son. He was extremely courteous to the young man, and finally succeeded in being invited to his father's house.

Ali Baba invited his son's new friend to stay for dinner, but the man refused.

"Why do you refuse?" said Ali Baba, surprised.

"It is because I can only eat food without salt, and this creates too much trouble for the people who invite me," said the phoney merchant.

"That makes no difference to me!" cried Ali Baba. "I can offer you a meal without salt. Come on! I beg you! Do me the honor and stay."

The man then accepted. Morgiane was annoyed that she had to start all over again, preparing food without salt, but she did as she was asked.

She thought the guest must be a very strange man to make such demands. Under the pretext of helping Abdalla, she served at the table so that she could have a look at the stranger.

Morgiane was more perceptive than Ali Baba. She recognized the cruel leader of the thieves straight away, even though he was disguised as a cloth merchant. She saw the knife he was hiding under his clothes and devised a very bold plan.

When they had eaten their dessert, she dressed herself up as a dancer, with a sword fixed to her belt as if it was part of the costume. Abdalla accompanied her playing the tambourine. As if it were part of the dance, Morgiane drew the sword from its sheath.

Ali Baba was delighted. He let her dance for a long time, thinking to entertain his guest who was actually waiting for the right moment to kill him.

As was the custom, when the dance was over, Abdalla took the hollow tambourine to collect some money.

Ali Baba threw in one gold piece, and the leader of the thieves took out his pouch to find one too. While he was fumbling in his pouch, Morgiane thrust the sword deep into his heart.

He died instantly.

Once again, Morgiane had uncovered the evil plot of the thieves' leader, and Ali Baba was determined to reward her richly.

A few days later, a magnificent feast was held to celebrate the wedding of his son and Morgiane.

Ali Baba let an entire year pass by, then as there appeared no reason to fear further reprisals, he mounted his horse and rode to the thieves' cave.

He cried out loud the words, "Open, Sesame!"

The door opened and Ali Baba found all the treasure as he had last seen it. Now he was the only one who knew the secret. He loaded his horse with gold and returned home.

At last he called his son and told him of his adventures from beginning to end, including the magic words.

And so this was how Ali Baba and his offspring passed the secret on from father to son. They lived in great splendor to the end of their days, and they were loved and honored by the entire city.

Tom Thumb

One evening, a poor farmer sat by the hearth poking up the fire to stir up some warmth. His wife sat next to him spinning thread.

"How sad it is that we don't have children!" he said. "Here it is always so quiet, while in the other houses it is noisy and lively."

"That is true!" sighed his wife. "If we only had one child, even if it were very tiny and not much bigger than my thumb, we would be satisfied and love it with all our hearts."

Now, it so happened that the wife's wish was granted. After seven months passed she gave birth to a child who was perfect in every way except that he was no bigger than her thumb.

"It is as we had wished it to be," she said. "He will be our dear child."

And because of his size, they named him Tom Thumb. Although he was given plenty of food, Tom did not grow any bigger, but stayed the same size as the day he was born. However, he had lively eyes and succeeded in everything he did because he was very intelligent.

One day the farmer was getting ready to go into the forest to cut wood.

"I wish that there was someone who could bring the cart to me," he said to himself.

"Oh father, I will take care of it," cried Tom Thumb. "You can rely on me! The cart will arrive in time in the forest."

The man started to laugh and said, "How can that be done? You are too small to lead the horse by the reins."

"That doesn't matter, father!" replied the lad. "If mother will harness it, I will sit in the horse's ear and tell him where to go."

"Thank Heavens!" he said. "I can spend the night in here safely." And he crept into the shell.

A little later on, when he was about to fall asleep, he heard two men pass by.

One of them said, "How shall we set about stealing the rich pastor's silver and gold?"

"I could tell you that," Tom Thumb shouted.

"What was that?" said one thief, trembling. "I heard a voice."

They stopped to listen, while Tom Thumb continued, "Take me with you. I will help you."

"But where are you?" they cried.

"Look on the ground and listen where the voice comes from," he answered.

The thieves found him at last and picked up the snail shell.

"Listen, little fellow, how do you think you can help us?" they said.

"Oh, I can climb into the pastor's room between the window bars, and hand out to you everything you want," replied Tom Thumb.

"Well, we will see what you can do," they decided.

Soon they arrived at the pastor's house and Tom Thumb slid into the room through the bars.

Tom's father picked up a pair of scissors, cut the wolf's stomach open and rescued his son.

"Thank goodness!" he said. "We have been so worried about you."

"Yes father, it is good to breathe fresh air again," replied his son.

"Where have you been then?" asked the man.

"Ah! father, I have seen much of the world. I have been in a mouse-hole, in a cow's stomach and in a wolf's belly. Now I am home with you which is where I want to stay."

"And we will never sell you again, not for all the treasures of the world," declared his parents.

They hugged their sweet Tom Thumb for a long time. And from that day on, Tom was far more careful about the journeys he made.

Aladdin
and the Magic Lamp

In the capital of an oriental kingdom lived a young boy called Aladdin. He was poorly dressed and he spent his days running barefoot through the streets with other rascals. He had lost his father, and it was his mother who had the job of feeding him. She earned money for food by spinning from sunrise to sunset.

"One day I will be old," she often said to him, "and you will have to work to earn your living. So learn a profession!"

But Aladdin laughed. "A profession? There's plenty of time for that! I'd rather enjoy myself!" And he ran outside to find his friends again.

Now, one afternoon, when he was playing in the town square, a man approached him. He was a stranger and, although Aladdin didn't know it, a great magician.

He said to the boy, "Would you like to become rich?"

"Of course!" said Aladdin. "But one has to work to earn money, and I prefer to play."

The magician smiled, "Work? What a thought! Be like me and you will have more treasures than a king!"

Aladdin trusted the magician and went with him.

First the man took Aladdin to a clothes merchant where he bought a magnificent outfit for him: a jacket embroidered with gold thread, a pair of shoes and a fur hat. In those days only the rich people wore such clothes.

"This is because you have to be smartly dressed to enter the place where I will take you," said the magician as Aladdin admired the outfit.

They walked for a long time, until they had crossed the entire city. Once they reached the countryside they finally stopped, right at the foot of a mountain.

Aladdin was still scared, but the magician gave him a ring and said, "This will act as a charm to protect you. If you do as I have said, you have nothing to fear. The second staircase leads to the orchard where you may pick all the fruit you want. But the most important thing that I want is a little lamp hidden in a secret place at the back of the orchard. Bring it to me!"

Aladdin hesitated, but the man pushed him inside. He went down the stairs slowly, step by step, holding his clothes tightly around him, terrified that he might accidentally touch something and be struck by lightning.

When he reached the foot of the stairs he crossed the three large halls without any difficulty. The last of these led him to the foot of a second staircase. Aladdin started to climb this staircase and eventually saw a light coming from the top.

Encouraged, he began to hurry...

When he reached the top he found himself in a fantastic garden with hundreds of trees full of shining fruit! However, this fruit was not meant for eating: the trees were laden with precious stones, sparkling diamonds, rich red rubies and milky pearls.

Poor Aladdin thought they were made of glass, like the cheap jewelry his mother wore. Nevertheless, he decided to pick some for her and began to fill his pockets. Then he saw the lamp standing in a hollow rock, and he remembered the reason for his visit. He stopped picking and ran towards it.

Lamps like this were to be found by the thousand in the East in those days and Aladdin did not understand why the magician wanted this one.

When he made his way back he found the stranger where he had left him.

"Do you have the lamp? Perfect!" the man cried.

Then he held out his hand and said, "Now give it to me. It will be much easier for you to climb the last few narrow steps without the lamp."

Aladdin saw the man's eyes light up with such greed that he did not trust him.

"No thank you, I can manage perfectly well!" he answered.

The magician insisted, but when he saw that Aladdin was not so easily led, he became very annoyed.

"How dare you disobey me!" he angrily. "This will cost you dearly!"

He poured the rest of the contents of the glass bottle over the fire and uttered some words that made the ground tremble. Before Aladdin could even go one step further, the opening closed!

The boy ran as fast as he could back to the stairs that led to the orchard, but that way was closed too!

"I have been caught like a rat in a trap!" groaned the boy, and collapsed on the stairs in tears.

Certain that he was destined to die all alone in this black hole, Aladdin fell asleep. For how long? That was difficult to say since no daylight came in.

When he woke up he was starving hungry and very cold. He rubbed his hands together to warm them up. As he was doing so, he also rubbed the ring that the magician had given him.

It did not take much rubbing before an extraordinary figure suddenly appeared from the ground. With his crooked hands, his long moustache and his dark eyebrows, he looked very fierce.

Nevertheless he said, "I am the genie of the ring. Your wish is my command. What do you want?"

"I want to get out of this place!" exclaimed Aladdin.

As soon as he made his wish, it was granted. The genie vanished and the cave opened. Aladdin was delighted and leapt outside, as free as a bird! Then, without losing any more time, he rushed home.

When his mother saw Aladdin she cried out with joy, "My child! My darling! I thought you were dead! Where have you been all this time?"

Aladdin told her what had happened to him and showed her the lamp, as well as the precious stones. His mother also thought they were made of glass. She did not give them another thought and put them in a box where they lay forgotten.

As for the lamp, she decided to sell it. Her starving son had eaten all the food in the house and with this she could buy some more bread.

She took a rag and polished the lamp… But two seconds later she dropped it on the floor and stared. A curious figure was standing in front of her, as terrifying as a demon. Nevertheless, when he spoke he sounded very friendly.

"I am the genie of the lamp," he said. "Tell me your wishes and they will be granted."

But it was Aladdin who spoke first: "We want something to eat!"

As soon as his wish was made, it was granted. The genie brought bread, two bottles of wine and all sorts of succulent food served on silver plates. There was enough for at least four meals!

Believe me, that night Aladdin and his mother went to sleep with full stomachs. And now that they knew how to make the genie appear, they were able to ask for everything they wanted. A soft touch with a rag on the lamp of happiness and, two minutes later, dinner was ready!

Soon they had more plates, forks and spoons than they knew what to do with, so they decided to sell them. They were made of silver, so they sold them for a good price. At last Aladdin and his mother had found a way to earn their living without getting tired!

The genie and the lamp kept them well for many years. As Aladdin grew up he lost his lazy attitude and took an interest in learning new things.

The rich merchants with whom he did business taught him good manners and the art of distinguishing glass from diamond.

At last he realized that the colourful fruits from the orchard were precious stones, and that he and his mother were, in fact, rich!

He was still counting all his wealth and wondering how to spend it, when something happened to interrupt his thoughts: Badroulboudour, the eldest daughter of the sultan and a princess of high rank, passed by his house.

Followed by her servants, she went to the bath house. She was renowned as a great beauty but, with a fan in her hand and a veil over her face, it was impossible to see whether it was true.

Aladdin, intrigued by the princess, followed her secretly. When they arrived at the bath house, Aladdin hid behind a door and stared. When the princess lifted up her veil the young man saw the most beautiful face he had ever seen. The next second he had fallen in love with her!

He ran home to his mother and told her everything. She thought he had gone mad, especially when he told her that he wanted to marry the princess.

"Marry her!" cried the good woman. "But her father is a rich sultan, and we, my child, are poor people!"

"Not any more!" replied Aladdin.

He went to look for the box in which lay the treasure from the orchard.

Taking it to his mother, he ran the jewels through his fingers and said, "They are real! Each diamond is worth more than all the silver plates we have sold. If you go to the palace with such a present, I am certain you will be admitted."

"To the palace!" cried his mother. "But I would never dare to do that! What would I say to the sultan?"

"That your son loves the princess and that he wants to marry her!" replied Aladdin. "Then you lay the present at his feet. Oh! I beg you, Mother, if you don't do it, I think I will die!"

Aladdin's mother was very frightened, but nonetheless she went to the palace the next day and knocked at the gate. She held the present close to her heart: a large cup containing precious stones and diamonds, covered with a white cloth.

She was reassured to see that she was not alone. Many people came to the palace, sometimes from afar, to ask the sultan for advice or a favor, and this happened almost every day.

After a while they were admitted, one by one. Aladdin's mother sat down in a corner and waited her turn. But when it came, she felt too shy to speak and ran away.

Aladdin groaned when he saw her come back, completely confused and still carrying the gift. She promised him that next day she would go to the sultan again.

Unfortunately, that day the sultan had gone out hunting and Aladdin's mother found the palace doors shut. Her son was so disappointed! He thought he was going to die of a broken heart!

The third day, however, his mother did get in to
see the sultan. He received her as he was sitting on
his majestic throne. Grandly he waved her closer
and she bent down low to kiss his feet.

"What can I do for you, my good woman?" he
asked.

The poor woman trembled and was too scared
to talk at first.

"Come, come! What is it?" he urged.

"Your Highness," she finally said, "I am afraid that my demand will not please Your Majesty… It is so insane, so senseless…"

"I order you: talk!" said the sultan who was becoming impatient with curiosity. "Whatever you ask me, you will be forgiven."

"Eh, well you see," she said, "it is my son, Aladdin… he has seen… he wants to…"

But instead of finally admitting the truth, she lifted up the cloth that covered the diamonds, and said, "He wants to offer you this modest present."

The sultan was startled: he had never seen such wealth!

Aladdin's mother took advantage of this and suddenly added, "My son loves your daughter. He is deeply in love with her and wants to marry her!"

Then she looked down at her feet, sure that the sultan would be furious and send her away…

But not at all! The treasure had such an effect on the sultan that he said, "Tell your son that my answer is yes!"

It is not hard to imagine Aladdin's joy that evening when his mother returned home. He was going to marry the sultan's daughter!

But the next morning he received a message from the sultan which read:

"*If young Aladdin wants my daughter's hand in marriage, he will have to bring me forty bowls filled with precious stones, pearls and diamonds, carried by forty servants.*"

"He has changed his mind," said the mother to her son. "I knew this would happen – he has found out that we are really poor! He doesn't want to admit that he broke his promise, so he asks you for things that you can't give."

"Eh well, that remains to be seen!" replied Aladdin, and he immediately looked for his magic lamp.

As soon as he rubbed it, the genie appeared.

"What do you want?" he said, gruffly.

Aladdin told him and two seconds later, all the forty servants appeared.

The little house suddenly became overcrowded. The servants looked splendid in their brilliant clothes, and on their heads they carried large silver bowls, filled to the brim with diamonds!

Aladdin commanded them to go to the palace to lay their treasures at the princess' feet. Then he said to his mother, "Go with them. You will bring me the sultan's answer."

When she came back from the palace after an hour, the good woman was crying. Aladdin was scared out of his wits, thinking they had failed… but she soon put him right.

"Don't look so sad, you silly, these are tears of joy!" she cried. "When the sultan saw the servants arrive, he did not have a second thought and cried out: 'Someone who can offer me so much wealth is worthy to marry the most beautiful princess!' I am so proud of you, my son!"

Aladdin was thrilled. He embraced his mother and danced her around the room.

"There is one little thing that worries me," she said at last. "The sultan's grand vizier alone was not happy. His son also had hoped to marry the princess. You will have to watch this man carefully in the future."

But Aladdin did not listen any more. He took the magic lamp and rubbed it.

When the genie appeared he commanded, "I want to take a bath!"

He had hardly pronounced these words when he felt himself lifted by invisible hands and plunged into an immense basin overflowing with perfumed water. What a marvelous bath! How good he felt! He came out clean and soft from head to toe.

Then he was dressed in magnificent clothes. When his mother saw him she cried out because he looked so handsome.

"This is only the beginning," he said, smiling. "The genie has promised me a hundred servants and a horse! And for you, dear Mother, thirty loyal servants!"

As soon as he had said these words everything appeared.

Aladdin had never ridden a horse before, but he mounted without any difficulty, for the genie had thought of everything.

"To the sultan's palace," he cried, urging the horse forward.

The horse obeyed and everyone followed him.

The people who saw this marvelous procession pass by could not believe their eyes, especially when the servants began to throw gold pieces in the air!

"Long live Aladdin!" cried the crowd, picking up the money.

Then the palace doors opened wide before him.

The sultan welcomed him. He was not disappointed with the look of his future son-in-law and neither was Badroulboudour.

She looked at Aladdin from behind some screens and fell immediately in love with him. She was at that time forbidden to show him her face: according to the oriental custom in those days, she had to keep it veiled until the day they married.

Aladdin talked with her father. Everything went well, and the sultan invited the young man and his mother to a magnificent feast.

"Glory to you, Aladdin!" he said, raising his glass. "You are worthy of my daughter and I give you her hand in marriage! When do you want the wedding?"

"As soon as I have built a palace beautiful enough for her to live in!" answered the young man.

"Well spoken!" said the sultan, and he emptied his glass.

That evening, at home, Aladdin's mother declared, "Explain it to me, my son, because I don't understand. For all this time you have been dreaming about just one thing: marrying the princess. Now, just as your dream comes true, you destroy everything by making a promise you can't keep! Have you gone mad?"

"Not at all," answered Aladdin, picking up the magic lamp.

Before the genie even had time to speak, Aladdin had already made his wish: a palace entirely made of marble, worthy of the princess. It should have walls decorated with diamonds, mosaic flooring, finished with everything of the finest quality, and surrounded by magnificent gardens!

The genie listened, not the least surprised. When at last he spoke it was to ask, "And where do you want this palace to be situated?"

"Opposite the sultan's palace," answered Aladdin.

"Very well," said the genie. And with that, he vanished.

The next morning, the genie appeared and said to Aladdin, "Your palace is built. Do you want to visit it?"

The young man was stupefied with this speed, but he nodded and a second later he was transported to the palace.

It was exactly as he had commanded... but ten times larger, ten times more astonishing and more dazzling! When he went inside, Aladdin noticed that numerous people were already busy: room maids, cooks, servants and guards. Everyone made a deep bow when they saw him pass.

He could see the sultan's palace from the front window. It was right across from his, as he had wished, with a long avenue in between. The princess could easily see her father every day, even after she was married. Aladdin was enchanted and thanked the genie warmly.

But someone in the sultan's palace wasn't pleased. Not the princess, of course, neither her nor her father. Indeed, when they woke up they both applauded at the sight of this miracle. No, the person who complained, protested, raged and sighed was the grand vizier.

"That palace isn't real!" he exclaimed to the sultan. "It is a magical trick! No one can build a palace in one night!"

"Magic or not, it's there!" replied the sultan. "Thanks to Aladdin who is rich and powerful! Whatever you think, he deserves the princess and he will marry her tomorrow!"

What was said was done. The marriage took place the next morning in the sultan's palace, and next evening the newly-weds moved into their magnificent palace across the way.

And so began a beautiful love story. The couple adored each other more and more every day, and Aladdin's mother, who lived nearby, got along very well with Badroulboudour.

Aladdin helped to govern the sultan's kingdom and, as time passed by, his subjects grew to love him more and more. Every time he went to the mosque or when he went hunting, he distributed gold pieces to the crowd. Everyone in the country spoke highly of his kindness, his generosity and his talent for keeping law and order.

He became so well known beyond the borders, the mountains and the seas that his name was even mentioned in Africa. There, lived someone who knew him very well, but who thought he had been dead for many years: the wicked magician!

He remembered the lad as if it were yesterday. If the poor Aladdin was rich now, it must be all thanks to the lamp he had found in the orchard. The magician promised himself to recapture it!

By means of magic he soon arrived in the East. There he swiftly disguised himself as a travelling merchant trading lamps. Then, finding out that Aladdin had gone hunting, he began to prowl around his palace.

As he was walking, he shouted, "Who wants to exchange an old lamp for a new one?"

Soon a window in the palace opened and a young servant appeared, waving a lamp. The magician recognized the magic lamp immediately. He was so happy that he left twelve others in exchange for this one. The servant called out many thanks, but the magician was already gone, carrying the lamp with him.

As soon as he was out of sight of the palace, he rubbed the lamp.

"Command, and I obey!" declared the genie when he appeared, for he had no choice.

"I want you to transport Aladdin's palace to Africa, as fast as possible," ordered the magician, "with everything inside and all the people that work in it!"

His wish was granted immediately, and just two minutes later the powerful genie flew off, carrying the magician, the palace and everything in it with him.

You can imagine poor Aladdin's face when he came home from hunting that night to find everything gone: no palace, no gardens, no furniture, no servants and, worst of all, no wife!

Frantic with worry, he ran like a madman to the sultan's palace.

"Ah, there you are, crook!" the sultan cried. "Where's my daughter? So, the grand vizier was right to curse your palace, saying it was just a magical trick! Well, my fine young beggar, you have forty-five days to redeem yourself. If my dear Badroulboudour still isn't back by then, you will be taken to the guillotine!"

Aladdin understood the sultan's anger and decided that he had better leave.

He crossed the entire city, looking everywhere for Badroulboudour, but no one had seen her. When he said that she had disappeared together with the palace, they thought he had gone mad.

He then went to the neighboring towns and, little by little, he searched the whole kingdom, but all in vain!

By the forty-third day, he was so tired and so desperate that when he saw a river, he decided to end it all. Just before he reached it, he slipped and fell.

Now, all these years he had been wearing the magic ring and forgotten all about it. When he fell, he rubbed the ring by accident and the genie appeared at once.

"Here I am, what do you want?" it asked.

"I want to see Badroulboudour again!" cried Aladdin.

The genie granted his wish on the spot. But to Aladdin's surprise, the genie took Aladdin with him to Africa.

There was his marvelous palace, stood like an immense green oasis in the middle of the desert.

He approached the nearest window and knocked on it gently. A few seconds later, the princess herself opened it!

She was so happy to see Aladdin again. She told him that she was a prisoner of the cruel magician who wanted to marry her against her will.

Aladdin was beside himself with joy to see her again. Nonetheless, he was confused.

"Why are you not surprised to see me here?" he asked.

"Last night I saw you in a dream," replied Badroulboudour. "Since then, I have been waiting for you. Come inside, I have a plan."

As soon as Aladdin was safely in the palace the beautiful girl told him her plan.

"At the moment the magician is not here," she said. "As soon as he comes back, you must hide. Tonight I will put a poison in his drink that a servant has bought for me. After that, it will be up to you to find us a way home again."

"That shouldn't be difficult!" cried Aladdin. "But first we will have to find a lamp that belongs to me and which must be in the hands of the wicked magician at this very moment."

He had hardly said this when a door slammed.

"There he is!" whispered Badroulboudour. "Quickly, hide yourself!"

Aladdin jumped into a clothes chest and she closed it after him. Time seemed to pass so slowly to the poor boy in his dark hiding place! Many questions went through his head, and he even wondered if Badroulboudour had miscalculated her plan. What if the deadly poison had no effect? What if the magician became suspicious and refused to drink?

The more the time went by, the more impatient he became and the faster his heart began to beat!

At last he heard footsteps and listened carefully. Did they belong to his wife or to the magician? Before he could give it another thought, the chest was opened: it was Badroulboudour! And she smiled at him!

"Come and see!" she cried.

He leapt out of the chest and walked behind her towards the dining room.

There he cried out with relief. The magician lay dead on the floor and the magic lamp stood next to him!

"I found it when I went through his pockets," explained the princess.

"Now, we are saved!" cried Aladdin.

Then Aladdin took the lamp and rubbed it. In less than a second the genie appeared.

"We want to return to our beautiful country!" cried the happy young man.

He had hardly pronounced these words when the palace and the gardens, the servants and the furniture, wife and husband, were all taken up by the powerful genie and flown back home.

When the sultan opened the grand palace shutters the next morning, a marvelous sight greeted his astonished eyes.

He was beside himself with joy when he saw that Aladdin's palace had returned. He didn't care a bit when the obstinate vizier repeated that it was just a magical trick, the sultan just hurried off to see his daughter.

Later on that day, a great feast was organized to celebrate Badroulboudour's and Aladdin's return, and if, amongst the laughter, one could sometimes hear some deep sighs, no one was surprised: it was only the grand vizier!

Rapunzel

Once upon a time there was a man and a woman who had wanted a child for a long time. Then, one day, the woman believed that her wish would be granted at last.

Their house had a little window at the back which looked out over a magnificent garden filled with beautiful flowers and all kinds of wonderful herbs and vegetables. The garden was surrounded by a high wall and no one dared to go in because it belonged to a powerful witch.

One day as the woman stood at the window and looked into the garden she noticed a bed full of splendid radishes which looked so fresh and so delicious that she longed to eat them. The longing to eat those radishes grew stronger day by day, and since this honest woman knew she could never have them, she grew thinner and became pale and weak.

Her husband became worried and asked, "What is the matter, my dear wife?"

"Alas," she said, "if I cannot eat some radishes from the garden behind our house, I will die!"

Her husband, who loved her very much, said, "I will not let you die, wife."

At dusk he climbed over the wall and went into the witch's garden where he hastily picked a handful of radishes and brought them to his wife. Immediately she made a salad out of them and greedily ate it. They tasted so delicious that the next day her desire for more was even greater.

To keep her contented, her husband knew he would have to be brave and go to the garden again. He waited until evening, when it began to get dark, but when he jumped down from the wall, he found himself face to face with the witch.

"How dare you come into my garden to steal my radishes," she said furiously.

"Alas!" he replied, "I did not come here by my own free will, but was forced to because of the danger that is threatening my wife. She saw your radishes from our window and had such a desire for them that she believed she would die if she could not eat them."

Then the witch said, "If everything you have told me is true, I will allow you to take as many radishes as you want. In return you must give me the child your wife will bear. The child will have a good home and I will be a mother to it."

The man was so terrified that he agreed to everything. When his wife gave birth to a little girl, the witch came to their home and took the baby away with her. She called her Rapunzel.

Rapunzel became the most beautiful little girl under the sun. When she was twelve years old, the witch locked her up in a tower in the middle of the forest. The tower had neither stairs nor doors, only a little window at the top. Every time the witch wanted to go to the top of the tower, she stood underneath and cried out:

"Rapunzel, Rapunzel,
Let down your hair!"

Rapunzel had wonderful long hair, as fine as spun gold. Whenever she heard the witch calling she unpinned her hair, fastened it around one of the window hooks and let it fall to the ground. Then the witch climbed up the golden rope.

It so happened that the king's son was riding through the forest one day. As he passed nearby the tower, he heard such a glorious sound that he drew up his horse to listen.

The beautiful sound was Rapunzel, trying to pass the time by singing. In vain, the prince looked for a door into the tower. However, the song had touched his heart so much that he returned to the forest every single day to listen to it.

One day he saw the witch come to the foot of the tower. The prince hid behind a tree to watch and heard her say:

"Rapunzel, Rapunzel,
Let down your hair."

Rapunzel then let down her long braids and the witch climbed up.

"So that is the way into the tower," he said to himself. "Well, I will just have to try my luck."

The next day at dusk, he went to the tower and called up:

"Rapunzel, Rapunzel,
Let down your hair."

Rapunzel's hair tumbled down immediately and the prince climbed up.

At first Rapunzel was terrified to see a strange man, but the prince told her gently that he had heard her sing and that his heart had been touched by her song.

Rapunzel then forgot her fears and the prince asked if she would have him for her husband.

She saw that he was young and handsome, and thought, "He loves me more than the old witch does." So she agreed, and gave him her hand.

The prince came to visit her every evening and the witch, who only came during the day, knew nothing at all about it.

Then, one day Rapunzel said without thinking, "Tell me, how is it that you are slow and heavy and pull my hair, whereas the prince climbs up to me so quickly?"

"You wicked child," cried the witch. "What is this I hear? So you have deceived me!"

In her rage she took Rapunzel's beautiful hair, wound it a couple of times around her hand and, snip! snap! she quickly cut it off. All the golden hair and the marvelous braids fell on the floor.

Then the witch took Rapunzel to a very remote place and abandoned her to live in loneliness.

That evening, as dusk fell, the witch hid herself in the tower. Soon the king's son arrived and called:

"Rapunzel, Rapunzel,
Let down your hair!"

When the witch heard this she fastened poor Rapunzel's hair to the window hook and let it fall to the ground. When the prince climbed up to the window he found this wicked witch instead of his sweet Rapunzel.

She looked at him with haunting, evil eyes and said, "Rapunzel is lost to you forever. You will never see her again!"

The prince was devastated. In his misery he fell from the window and landed in a bramble bush. He was not killed, but the thorns on the bush made him blind.

Unable to think of life without Rapunzel, the young man wandered into the forest. He lived on berries and roots, and drifted in this way for many years, until one day he arrived by chance at the lonely place where Rapunzel lived in misery.

All at once he heard a voice that was familiar to him and walked towards the sound. When he was close, Rapunzel recognized him. She was over-joyed to see him, but sad when she noticed his sightless eyes. She put her arms around his neck and wept.

Two tears fell from her eyes into the eyes of the blind prince. Instantly they became clear again and he could see as he did before. Then, happily reunited with his love, he carried Rapunzel to his kingdom where they married and lived happily ever after.

Beautiful Vassilissa

Once, in a kingdom far, far away, there lived a merchant and his wife. They had one daughter who was called Beautiful Vassilissa.

When the girl was eight years old, her mother became very ill. One day she called her daughter to her side.

"Listen, my child," she said, "and remember the last words I have to say. I am going to die, my dear. I give you my blessing and this little doll. You must always keep it with you and never show

233

it to anyone else. If ever you are in trouble, just ask the doll for advice."

Then the mother embraced her daughter and died.

The merchant grieved for a long time after his wife's death but, as time passed, he began to think about marrying again. He was a real gentleman and many women admired him. There was one widow of whom he was very fond. She had two daughters of about the same age as Vassilissa and was considered by everyone to be a good mother.

Then, one day the merchant married the widow, but he had been deceived because she was not a good mother at all to his daughter, who was the most beautiful girl in the village.

The woman and her daughters were extremely jealous of Vassilissa's beauty. They treated her very badly and made her do the dirtiest housework, hoping that the hard work would make her pale and ugly.

However, Vassilissa did all the work without complaining, and every day she became more and more beautiful. Her sisters, although they never lifted a finger to help, became scrawnier and uglier because of their envy.

But how did this happen? It was all thanks to the doll that protected Vassilissa. It comforted her when she was unhappy, gave her good advice and helped her with the housework.

Several years passed by in this way until Vassilissa had reached the age to be able to marry. All the young men of the city asked for her hand in marriage, but no one ever thought about asking the other daughters.

Their angry mother always said to the suitors, "I will never consent to a marriage of the youngest daughter before the two older ones are married!"

Then, when she had driven away the suitors, she would turn and slap Vassilissa angrily.

One day the merchant went away on business to another kingdom. At once the woman moved into a different house near a dense forest. In the middle of this forest was a clearing with a small hut in which lived a witch. If anyone dared to come near the hut she would eat them, as if they were chickens!

The woman constantly sent Vassilissa into the forest on different pretexts, hoping the witch would rid her of the girl. But Vassilissa always returned home safe and sound because the doll showed her the way home and warned her when the old witch was near.

One evening, the woman ordered all three daughters to do some work. One was to make lace, one was to knit stockings, and Vassilissa was to spin. Each of them had a certain amount to do before going to bed. The woman then put out all the lights in the house, leaving only one candle burning for the girls. Then she went to bed.

The young girls started their work by this poor light. After a while the candle began to flicker. One of the sisters took a snuffer and pretended that she was going to trim the wick; instead she put the candle out on purpose.

"What are we going to do?" the girls cried. "There are no more matches to light the candle and our work is not finished. Someone will have to go to the old witch in the forest to ask for a light."

"I have enough light from my needles, so I won't go," said the one who was making lace.

"Neither will I," said the one who was knitting. "I have enough light from my needles too."

"You will have to go to find a light," they cried to Vassilissa. "Go to the witch."

Then they pushed Vassilissa out of her chair and told her to go.

The girl went into her room, gave some food to her little doll and said, "Dolly dear, eat this food and listen carefully to me. My sisters are sending me to the old witch and she will eat me."

"Don't be afraid," replied the doll. "Go where they send you, but take me with you and you will have nothing to fear."

Vassilissa put the doll in her pocket and walked bravely into the dense forest. As she was walking, a sudden breeze made her whole body shiver.

Then a horseman passed at full gallop in front of her; his face was completely white, and he was dressed all in white. To her surprise, it became light.

Vassilissa continued walking. Just then another horseman passed by her. This man's face was red, he was dressed in red and he sat on a red horse. To her surprise, the sun rose.

The girl walked on and on, until at last she arrived in the clearing where the old witch's little hut stood. It was circled by a fence made of human bones, and on top of the fence sat a row of skulls. On the door she saw a human bone which served as a bolt, and instead of a lock there was a human jawbone.

Vassilissa stopped walking for she was paralyzed with fear. Just then a third horseman arrived. His face was black and he was dressed in black, riding on a black horse. He rode up to the door of the old witch's hut and disappeared, as suddenly as if he had sunk into the earth.

Then it became night, but the darkness did not last for long because the skulls' eyes on the fence started to shine.

Vassilissa was still frozen with terror. She did not know what to do and stood there like a statue.

All at once there was a terrible noise in the forest; the trees shook their branches and the dry leaves rustled, and then the old witch appeared.

When she reached her doorstep, she stopped, sniffed the air and cried, "Mmmm! I smell a child! Who is it?"

Vassilissa went to the witch, curtsied and said, "It is I, Madam! My sisters have sent me here to ask for a light, for we have no matches at home."

"Good," said the witch, "I know them and I will give you the light. First, however, you must work for me for a while."

Then she turned to the door and cried, "My solid bolts, lift yourself; my door, open yourself!"

The door opened and the witch went inside, while the wind whistled through the house.

When she reached her room, the witch sat down at the table and said to Vassilissa, "Serve me everything that is in the oven, I want to have my dinner here!"

Vassilissa lit a candle by holding it against one of the shining skulls on the fence. Then she took the food from the oven and served it to the witch. She also went to the cellar to get some ale, beer and water. It was enough for ten men.

The witch ate and drank everything. All she left was a drop of cabbage soup and a small piece of bread.

Then the witch went to bed, saying, "While I am out tomorrow, you will clean the courtyard, sweep the rooms, make lunch and do the washing. Then you must go to the shed, where you will find a pile of wheat, and get rid of the beetles. Make sure that everything is done before I come home or I will eat you!"

When she had finished speaking, the witch fell asleep and began to snore.

Vassilissa gave the rest of the food to her doll, and in tears she said, "Dolly dear, eat this food and listen carefully to me. The old witch has told me to do an impossible amount of work and she will eat me if I have not finished in time."

The doll replied, "Don't be afraid, beautiful Vassilissa. Have your dinner and go to sleep. The night will bring an answer."

Very early the next morning Vassilissa got up and looked out of the window. The eyes of the skulls had stopped burning. Then the white horseman passed in front of her and it was light.

The old witch left the house and whistled. Her mortar, pestle and broom appeared at once. Then the red horseman rode by and the sun came out. The witch sat in her mortar and went off, driving it with the pestle, while she swept away her tracks with the broom.

Vassilissa took the chance to walk around the house and admired the witch's wealth. She wondered what part of the work she should do first, but when she looked again, she noticed that the work was already done! And that was not all – the doll had removed the beetles from the wheat!

"Oh, my good helper," said Vassilissa "You have saved me!"

"You only have to prepare dinner, and there's plenty of time for that," answered the doll as she climbed back into Vassilissa's pocket.

In the evening, Vassilissa set the table and waited for the witch to return. When it started to get dark, the black horseman appeared in front of the door and immediately it became completely dark. Only the skulls' eyes glittered in the night.

Suddenly the trees started to shake and the leaves began to rustle. The old witch was coming. Vassilissa went to meet her.

"Is everything done?" asked the witch.

"Look for yourself, Madam!" replied the girl.

The witch looked around her. She was very annoyed that she could not find any faults.

"All right, Vassilissa!" she said. "This time you have done the work."

Then she cried, "My faithful servants, devoted friends, come and grind the wheat!"

Out of nowhere, three pairs of hands appeared, grabbed the wheat and took it away.

Once again the witch ate to her heart's content. Before she went to sleep, she said to Vassilissa, "Tomorrow you must do the same as you did today. However, you must also take the pile of poppies from the shed and wipe off the dust."

Having said this, she turned over to face the wall and started to snore.

As she had done the night before, Vassilissa asked her doll for advice.

The doll answered, "Don't worry, go to sleep. The night will bring an answer. Tomorrow you will see that everything has been done."

The next day, when the witch had left, Vassilissa and her doll once more shared the tasks.

When the witch came back that night, she was again annoyed to find no faults when she examined everything.

Then she cried, "My faithful servants, devoted friends, press the oil out of the poppies."

Out of the air, three pairs of hands arrived at her command, gathered the poppies and took them away. Then the witch ate her dinner, while Vassilissa stood in front of her in silence.

"Why don't you say anything?" asked the witch. "Have you lost your tongue?"

"If you allow me, I would like to ask you something," said Vassilissa.

"Ah! Ask if you like, but you should know that not every question leads to something good!" cackled the witch. "Remember, if you know a lot, you soon become old."

"I would like to ask you three questions," said Vassilissa. "On the way to your hut, I was passed by a horseman with a white face, wearing white clothes and riding a white horse. Who is this man?"

"He is my daylight," replied the witch.

"Then I saw another horseman who had a red face," continued the girl. "He was dressed in red and riding a red horse. Who is he?"

"He is my beautiful sun," answered the witch.

"And the black horseman I saw near the door?" finished the girl.

"He is my dark night," said the witch.

Vassilissa remembered the three pairs of hands, but did not ask anything more.

"No more questions?" asked the witch.

"I know enough for now," replied the girl. "You said yourself that a lot of knowledge makes you grow old too soon."

"That is true," said the witch. "I don't like

revealing my secrets to the world. But now, I will ask you a question. How did you manage to finish all the work I gave you?"

"My mother's blessing has helped me," answered Vassilissa truthfully.

"Ah! So that is the reason!" cried the witch. "Then you must leave this house at once, blessed girl. I don't like blessed girls!"

She grabbed Vassilissa's wrist and dragged her out of the room, then pushed her outside.

She then took one of the skulls with shining eyes from the fence, put it on a stick and gave it to Vassilissa.

"Take this, it's the light for your sisters," she said. "Take it home."

At once Vassilissa started to run and the light from the skull guided her.

After a long journey, she reached home again. When she went into the house, the skull said, "Don't throw me away, take me to the woman!"

For the first time ever, Vassilissa was welcome in the house. Since she had left, the woman and her daughters had been living in the dark. They had not been able to light a match, and any light they took from their neighbours went out as soon as they entered the room.

"Perhaps, your light will not go out," they cried, grasping the stick from her.

They carried the skull into the room and its burning eyes stared at the three women. It didn't matter where they tried to hide, it seemed that they were followed everywhere by its haunting look.

By the morning, they had all been burnt to ashes; only Vassilissa survived.

The next day Vassilissa buried the skull, locked the house and went to town to find work. An old lady asked for her companionship, and so she stayed there, waiting for her father to arrive.

One day, she said to the old lady, "I am very bored staying in the house all day with nothing to do. Please, buy me some flax and I will pass the time spinning."

"The old lady bought her some flax and Vassilissa began to spin. She worked so well that the thread came out as smooth and fine as a hair.

When she had spun a large pile of thread, Vassilissa wanted to start weaving it. The doll then gave Vassilissa a magnificent loom, suitable for weaving such fine thread. By the end of the winter, the cloth was finished and it was so fine that it could be threaded through the eye of a needle.

In the spring she bleached the linen and said to the old lady, "Please, sell this piece of cloth and keep for yourself whatever money it fetches."

"But my child," gasped the lady, "only the king is worth such a cloth! I will take it to the palace."

"What is it you want, dear woman?" asked the king when he saw her there.

"Your Highness," she answered, "Forgive me, but I have brought something wonderful to show to you."

When the king saw the cloth, he was also amazed. "What do you want for it?" he asked.

"Your Highness, this cloth is priceless," replied the lady. "I brought it as a gift."

The king thanked her and showered her with rich gifts in return.

"I would like shirts made from this cloth," declared the king. "But who can sew such finery?"

The king searched the land for such a needle-worker, but all in vain. Then he sent for the old lady again.

"If you have been able to spin and weave this cloth, you should also be able to sew it," he said.

"This cloth was not my work," she replied. "It was a young girl who made it."

"Well then, let her sew the shirts," ordered the king.

And so, the old lady went home and told the whole story to Vassilissa. At once she locked herself in her room and began to work night and day.

Soon a dozen shirts were finished and the good lady took them to the king.

It wasn't long before Vassilissa saw the king's servant standing at the door, saying, "His Majesty wants to see with his own eyes the girl who made his shirts. He wants to reward her in person."

Vassilissa set off for the palace and presented herself to the king, who, as soon as he saw her, fell head over heels in love with her.

He took beautiful Vassilissa's white hands and sat her next to him on the throne. That very day they were engaged to be married.

Soon afterwards her father came back from his long journey. He was delighted with his daughter's fate and made his home with her. Vassilissa also welcomed the old lady, who had given her shelter, into the palace and, of course, the dear doll stayed by her side forever after.